Bottomless

T.R. Horne

VB
YOSHIMA BOOKS

Printed in the United States of America
First Printing, 2016

ISBN-13: 978-0-9911063-8-7
ISBN-10: 0-9911063-8-5

Ordering Information: Special discounts are available on quantity purchases. For details, inquire at the website below.

Yoshima Books www.yoshimabooks.com
Book Design by Polgarus Studio
Cover Design by VamosWrite.com

For the Fear of Love

Contents

Note from Author

When I think of love and relationships, I think of how difficult it can be to mesh two people together. People that are raised in different households, with different cultures and different values. Different desires. If you're lucky, you find that one. You know, the one that fits your crazy. This poetry book is a culmination of stories spanning a fifteen year period of dating, loving, using men and attempting to understand the opposite sex. It examines the bottomless efforts we pour into finding the right person. Some poems are the stories of close friends. Don't ask me which because I'll never tell. Their secrets are safe in my vault. You'll find some humor, some thought-provoking, and some heart-wrenching pieces. But most importantly, you'll find me…and hopefully, you'll find yourself there too.

Enjoy the journey.

Bottomless

Where Do I Begin

Where do I begin?
It started back when
I was still young and wanting more, more
Dance moves, more slow grooves
And definitely
I wanted to be innocently
Brought to a simple juxtaposition
Of adolescence and independence.

I wanted to sit at the big table
Open my eyes during the nasty part
And be creative
Like my big brother.

I was a shadow.

An illusion to the looking glass
And that's how I passed
Into a young adult role.
I wasn't quite ready to release, unfurl
And become the monstrosity of
My father's heart and mother's dream.

See, she wanted me
To stay away from those retched knuckleheads
Because all they want
Is something that can take them
Back to wetting the bed
But without the urine smell.

I wanted to be held.

To be wanted
Like the big titty girls,
Thick, dark girls,
And those curly head mulattos.
I wanted this, that and those
I wanted to be known
Cause' I was just a sad mistake
With thick glasses instead of
A thick ass
And big teeth
Instead of titties.

It was a shame
That the only ones who knew my name
Were the teachers and the lunch lady
I was never the crush

Never the tease
So I aimed to please…mentally.

And I grew
And grew
Until I was able to get phone calls from young gents
That claimed they had…it…all.
One played basketball
And he was my first chance
At something like romance.
Yeah, it was generic.
We never talked in public
And he never could grasp a subject
Outside how much snap in his wrist
Would get the ball to go in.

So we didn't last.

Well, until after his birthday, of course.
Because he knew I had an allowance and a giving
heart
That could keep us together for a while longer.
And then something spectacular happened
Must have been a cloud cleared
Over my nappy head and unshaved legs,

I grew.
And grew.
And became the essence of woman.

I was like the flavor
Of the greatest, juiciest steak
I was reinvented as
A woman.
Worth something more
Than a menial thrill.
I was pretty and it felt
Surreal to be finally wanted and craved.
My beauty was the equivalent of outstanding grades,
Straight A's…and everything was alright.
Until that night.

I met a man beneath
The Venus moon
That would soon steal what
Many men had asked for in prayer
And I was no longer inexperienced
But instead
I was steering a vessel I couldn't control.
As time went on,
I became an expert pilot

With scarlet ways and crimson ambition
I…had…it…all.
Brains, beauty and brawn
And my tough past
Came to me in nightmares
They were like photos
Of times I wished I could erase
But we all know photos last a lifetime,
And so do my memories.
They plagued me.
Taunted me when it was time to speak
Time to be noticed in society
I still heard them chanting, "Sticks!"
On the red dodgeball court
At my thin brown frame.
I ran as far away as the edge would allow
And blocked out the voices that
Still followed.

And here I am
Young, Successful and Beautiful
And totally
Unforgiving and
Focused.

Kindred Spirits

He said we were kindred spirits
That we all walked the same plain
But see,
I was hypnotized by the way he
Licked lips
Dipped hips
And rubbed the small of my back.
So I was led to believe in
Kindred spirits.

We talked about life's trials
And its acquittals
We delved in fantastic tragedies
That graduated to him
Laying me…
Mentally.
It was like he
Appeared from dim dreams
And was precisely cut from
My seams
Perfectly fitting all of me.

But like the moon swivels and the Earth tilts
We moved with it, except
He had a different rotation.
He wanted dance clubs and hot women
I wanted jazz sets and cool men
So then
The story proceeds
As a movement,
A gesture, of things
We'd already seen
It was just in fast forward
The remote control was broken
But I had no idea who kept clicking
Past my greatest times like my favorite shows.
Our first kiss
Click!
Our first dance.
Click!
Our first romance.
Click! Click! Click!

It was rounding the bend
Erasing the future
I'd so carefully drawn in pen
Because we were kindred spirits

Like he had once said.
I was dumb to hear it
And believe it
As we slept between moist sheets and
Crept around dark, slick streets
To be together
To be forever.
Our kindred spirits were hidden so deep
Behind the perceived faithfulness of his lying eyes.

The Last Night

Make love to me
Grind your hands
Until you feel the pain
In my joints,
Massage the bone
I want to feel you, all
Every last centimeter
You have to give
Don't fall
Just let me feel your emotions
I want to hear them moan
For my curves
Hear them scream for me
To let my guard down.

Make love to me.
Like I'd die tomorrow
Before you could kiss me awake
Like the last time has already started.
Grab my shoulders
Pull me into you
Until every valley touches every hill.

Wrap your legs with mine
Until we slither
On the carpet
Burning our backs
But not noticing all the same.
We play games
With each other's mouths
We kiss tongues
And suck swollen lips.
We feel the warmth
Of being two as one.

Make love to me
With your eyes open
Can you see what I'm thinking?
I want you here
Yes, right there.
Flowing with my motion
It's like we're dancing over a jazz beat
We've created a silhouette
Of black beauty.
We are like sun and moon,
We exist together.
Two entities with the same motivation.
Make love to me,

Like we were best friends
Since grade school
And you dreamt of this night
Since 1986 to 1996
And now were indulging in
What was always meant to be.
I want to make love
And give all my hurt and pain
All my joy and happiness
Into those hands
That rub them all away.
I'm neither happy nor sad
Just content.
And willing to remain in nothingness
At least until you

Make love to me
Like I'd die tomorrow
Before you could kiss me awake.

Tic-Tac-Toe Life

A tic-tac-toe life
Everyone waiting on the next move
Deciphering what their opponent
Will do
Or can do
To conquer the game.
Surmising what move to make
Taken by the challenge of winning
And the underlying fear of loss.
We all fall victim to the
Checkerboard, battleship, spade or monopoly
Hoping we're not failing when
We miss a piece,
A chance,
An opportunity.
Fighting, spitting and grappling
To earn the title that lasts until
You're overthrown
Or tire of overcoming.
Fun is now underfoot
Duty is the honor in it all
Becoming obsessed and overzealous

With stamina, endurance and fame
Things that all fade with time
And we, then, lose
The purpose of the game.

For the Poet in You

This is for the poet in you.

Words a gift, unwrapped
Trapped inside your mind
Can't realize how to define
The emotions, the tactical wave
Of feelings…overactive and
Dehydrating your lips, your throat
Your vessel of what's internally
Scrawled throughout your soul.

This is for the poet in you.

Pen ink like air or water
Breathing life into pages
Getting them nourished and healthy
To feed the masses.
Poet, teacher, student, thinker
Define the fine line of who you are
Or want to be
Through green lines etched on once
Green trees

The smell like nature after a rain
Right there with you in your safest place
Feel at one with yourself, the natural you
Happily exalted in pleasurable pain
As you write
From the poet in you.

Stage Personality

Skating on the convenience of the hour
Lasting off a lioness cowering
Bending for the blows
Dodging what? No one knows.
Escaping through poetry and prose
Taking it slow
Behind the mic, my feelings sweat
In front of the crowd, they're drowning in depth
Caressing my stage fright
Cross your legs, be polite
They say
No split tresses or skirts
No halfway shirts
Just the pinkness of my femininity
And blackness of my negativity.
They hear the violent tone
That thumps their ears
Hugs their tears and quiets the yell of their fears
They hear the words
Through my thick skin
Words like phrases of pollution...
Everyone will suffer eventually.

The black zone, ozone, twilight zone
Whichever zone suits you
Submerge, naked and unashamed.
Hit with a C4 blast of reality
That what they want, isn't what they hear
Your life story
The struggles
The tears
Mean nothing.

Unashamed

Does anybody hear you?
When you think
Or do they just smile…
As you sink further?
You feel so alone
That you can't tell the secret
That your souls without a home
A place of security
A touch of Fate
As you try to relate
To people that don't understand
The underlying feelings,
Not the smile you paint on
Or the frown you cement upside down.

Does anybody hear you?
When you think
Or do they just smile…
As you fake
To be someone acceptable
Presentable, meek and approachable
The mask, like clothes, you're naked without it.

The mirror, your self-empowerment, is now covered
Like your personality,
No one likes the real you
But the new you
Is much better, maybe easier
To get along with
Because that other girl...
Was too nonchalant, too unpredictable, too opinionated.
You've cloned yourself
Without the personality
So maybe they'll be happier.
They'll nod their heads
Give the thumbs up
And you're thrust into society
Like a baby...head first
And ignorant.
You'll use your senses
And wear the lenses that make you look smart
Clothes that make you appear sexy
When all it is
Is naked.
Naked truth
About how you changed
Just to be unashamed.

Story of the Soul

It just doesn't make sense
Me sitting here
Your eyes intense
Staring deeper
Into a creature
That is like a lioness
Mysterious and curious
Quick and vicious
Licking lips, for the food
Of thought is nourishment.
The words tasty as
Momma's fresh pound cake
With the strawberry flavor
Of her femininity
Coating like caramel topping
With the cherry of newness
Propped gleaming on the peak.
You listen when she opens up to speak.
She's difficult but interesting
A noble subject for the taking
If only you could wrap her
In your strong grip

But like wet soap, she slips
From your grasp
Then slants her head and asks
Is that all you got?
She's a vixen, never giving in
Or sitting when she'd rather stand
Timid, sensitive internally
Rigid, commanding externally
Her cocoa eyes, shapely thighs
And exotic features
Back up her threats
Of constant pleasures.
So when you bow down to her essence
She stuns you with
Long lasting lovemaking
Thought provoking
Shivering, spinning
Spasms of orgasmic geysers.
She knows the look in her eyes
Have shown her life story
As she rises and falls in glory
Standing inches away
She whispers so softly,
"We'll meet again."
And you believe her

As she walks out, leaving you…
Wondering.

Temptations

Your glance rolls over my body
Like glaze on a soft doughnut
Getting lost in my firm thighs,
Cocoa eyes and moist lips.
His head bobs with my hips
Watching the curve in my back
Fantasizing about how he could,
Um, do that thing to me, that
He does to make me...*mmm*.

He says

So here we are
In a place that prohibits
The ecstasy of temptations
So easily manipulated am I
By a tender kiss in the wind
Or wink of her exotic eye.
Impossible to be so deeply
Smitten by the purr of her
Physically restrained kitten.

But he hears it purr.

In her mannerisms
Saw it in her voice

And tasted it with her look.
Damn, she had him confused.
Mixing up adverbs
Forgetting the verbs
Can't contain his thoughts
Of smelling her exotic juices
Fluent and dripping
Mm-hmm, that's what he's tasting
As he sees her dancing in the distance
Tempting him.

Angels & Demons: Messengers

Raging, screaming from Hell
Through the depths they rise and prevail
Giving greed to the untidy
Strength to the powerless
And the weak the corner to fight.
It's like
You've lost sight
Of when or where they came from
Woke up one day and they were there
Breathing heavily
Eyes the portholes of destruction
Scoured the mansions to inner city corruption
Claiming souls and bodies
To carry a message to the unsuspecting.
They visit the homes of mothers,
Fathers and friends…well wishing
Smiling beneath a mask of envy
Knowing that we're all privy
To temptation.
A festive mask for the manipulation
Perfect for the occasion
They've planted the seed of ignorance.

By ignoring the stance
It takes to fight a vision
We can't place as human or indecent.
You fall,
Hypnotized as we apologize
In prayer.
Forgiven yet sleeping in their lair.
All forgotten but who's not being fair?
They know your thrills and chills
And stop at nothing to fulfill
Your pagan dreams
Or greed.
And in the event
That the weak should break free
The wrath exposed
Is nothing short of minor league
Your homes, family and lives
Are at stake
We see the plan, we know the date.
It's like you've fallen in a stupor
Without ever getting a chance to wake.
But in their eyes, the job is done.
The mission collapsed
Provoking you no longer fun
They leave your soul for us to reconstruct

To give it the spine, blood and pulse
Massage your brutalized mind
With unconditional love
Deranged and completely giving in
To trust
We take your soul…
Because you're giving it to us.

Midnight Call

You thought you were clever
By innocently inviting me over
I knew what would follow
As we had no conversation
None worth remembering anyhow
So as we fall to the carpet
By the fire
Shed our attire
And share glances at our anatomy
I'm not thinking of the truth, you see
I'm dazzled with my fantasies
Never mind you're manipulating me
Because the way your warm hands
Spread warm oil on my oh so warm skin
Has my eyes closed, withdrawn in
Ecstasy.
And this isn't feeling like an attack.
The candles answer rhetorically
As my moan questions against the crackle of wood
I hear the steady hum of your heartbeat
The tremble in your touch
I feel the wetness in your tongue

Tasting my flavor

Smelling my scent on your body and then…

There's an ending.

And nothing more.

Desire

I knew he was smooth
From the way he strolled through
Enticing fantasies and lust
I was imagining a nut bust
When he sat calmly across from me
It was his eyes, you see
That bore holes through me, into me
I shook away my lascivious thoughts
Like a dog in the rain
He was
Intellectual, successful and beautifully
Innocent
And not fit to be slain.
Ditching predatory thoughts
We mind fucked.
And he was wild and untamed
Like a bronco he bucked
As I held on to the reins
Pulling him deeper down mental alleyways.
The darkness didn't dissuade
I knew it because he leaned back
Assessed

Then prepared for the attack.
I am skilled in the art of defense.
So once our encounter was minced
By the time or the place
Or the waiter awaiting his pay
We both sucked the steam between us
To a simmer
And on this 10:15pm
Cold winter, middle of December evening
We exchange competitive, unrelenting
Desire.

Stimulation

He sits silently
Not speaking
But it's interesting
Watching him nervously
Picking his nails
Wondering if time will let him prevail
The air gets stale
As he eyes my glance
The future plays like a reel
Of the greatest movie until
I smile his way.
The ease of conversation
Smooths the features of his face
And we're careening past outer space
Frolicking with goddesses
Not realizing we've left this place
And did 180 degrees of discussion
Led by the orchestra
Pounding with the percussion.
It's like waves as he dances mentally
I keep thinking I may be drowning
Then remember that I'm still breathing

Enlightened.
The passions heightened
Then time rewinds and gives second chances
Through flirtatious glances
"We shouldn't be here," I whisper.
So softly he can't hear
I devour his emotional food
And emerge full.
Now he leans back in his chair
Kicks off his shoes
Gets comfortable in my lair,
My den, my space, my haven
I could get used to this idea.
He laughs to hide the underlying discomfort
Of leaving my solitary lifestyle behind
For a man that stimulates my mind.

Artistry

Let me draw you
At least let me think I can

I'll shape the almond eyes to perfection
Show the reflection in its irises.
I'll shape the slope of your nose
Into the hills of your cheekbones
And give that smirk its justice.
It's a love game through my charcoal
And fingertips
It's like I can feel you form
As you grow
From each lonely feature
Into the beauty and elegance
Of something extraordinary
A creature
Of expressive faces, full lips
Faithful grins

Let me draw you
At least let me think I can

I've grown to know you
At nights when I can't sleep
Days when I think they'll never end
I see you, half done, incomplete
And I smudge you deeper in
Into me
I feel the depth of you in its blackness
Etching the uniquely flawed features
With precision and care.

Let me draw you
At least let me think I can.

Familiar Stranger

Did he notice me
Before or after
I acted like I couldn't see him
Or sense him near me?
Why so nonchalant?
So laid back
Assuming I'll attack the conversation with vigor?
Things changed
While I was away
They say
He's been ingesting some sweet rose
Yet profoundly no one knows
That we shared
Long nights talking about family
With melodies surrounding us like
We were living in fantasies
He kissed the back of my knee
Did they know that?
I remember
His hands slipped up the slope of my spine,
Across trembling shoulders still
Unsure about it, him and us

His breath swept my neck
I felt the erectness…
But we sit like strangers in public
Catch eyes that hide passionate nights
He smirks, I smirk, and we flirt
Through distant glances
Keeping our distance for the masses
Because they watch so closely
And for the sake of his new relationship
And my internal hardships,
We walk away strangers
With an interlaced past.

Back in Town

I've been calling around
Wondering if you're lost,
Can't be found…in your usual habitat.
Checked the café where we drank lattes
And laughed at ancient memories.
Went by the spot at that place
That you said makes you feel calm and poetic.
Guess you haven't felt focused
Enough to visit.
Your friends say that all is well
But your numbers kind of sketchy
Hard to tell.
So I sit alone, at home, listening
To jazz greats that once made
Candles belly dance on dark walls.
The saxophone still reminds me of that
Thing you did with your lips
That had me laughing and moaning
Without even a touch from your fingertips.
You told me not to run
Because you wouldn't chase.
You told me to open my eyes

Don't hide my face.
I had smiled then
Felt reassured when
The cuddling turned to confessing
But I sit here alone with promises
And a lukewarm latte
Hoping that someone tells you I'm looking
To see you, hoping to meet you…again.

Creative Registration

Creatively, I have registered near wealth
And physically, I see no one better than myself
But I'm in limbo between
Confusion on if I'm truly complete
And of the depth of greatness in how I see me.
It's honestly not conceit.
Just high self-esteem.
Because I know my history, my strength
I know my depth, my weight, my range
In societies view on things.
I am a queen.
I was a princess as an adolescent.
Now I'm in charge of
How I love, who I love
And what I love, right?
Absolutely, completely, totally
Wrong.
No matter my maturity, I'm still docile
In my attempts to be more than a physical
satisfaction
For a man
A mental lapse in judgement

Or a stain on everything great with this world.
I can be more!
More laughs than
All your childhood rolled into one
More intellect than a book could share
More ambition than your dreams could draw out
More woman than you've ever held and caressed
I can be more!
If you let me.

The Performance

I watched you on stage
Doing your thing
Smirking at the edge of sentences
And sometimes a paraphrase

I wanted you then.

As your voice rose in rage
And whispered beneath emotion
It was a misleading contradiction
That made me think of sexual advances
Caught imagining how you'd be
Romantic and slow or
Rough and sensual
As you rocked the mic
I envisioned my thighs
Rocking, bumping and grinding into you
As I ride.
Your hands trembled when you paused
I waited for you…to continue.
Sitting on the edge of your words like
I was waiting on the number nine bus to arrive

I like the way the spotlight
Illuminates your deep, brown eyes
Or the way your dark chocolate skin glows
With the glaze of sweat
Nervousness.
I was feeling you
As you were feeling *it*
Your voice hoarse
I clear the lump in my throat.
We have performed elegantly.

I Can Float

I can float like the sturdiest eagle over the Colorado River to the Mississippi and the Nile. In my fantasies I can be who I want. No rules, regulations or expectation. The comfort of being alone without feeling lonely. No need to speak or think because all my thoughts are reality. My daydreams dance with life. The music smiles and the sun sparkles like multicolored gems. The clouds are scented pillows and the roads are always empty. The stars no longer twinkle but careen to Earth as diamonds just for me. I trade talent with the unspeaking people. We speak only through our dancing, carving and instruments. We exist in each other's happiness.

Like every good fantasy, I awake.

The sun shines down in scorching heat, cars push past rudely. The flowers aren't growing but no one stops to realize it. They wake up daily to pay the bills and buy more this or that. New clothes, new cars, bigger house, more social value. The have's and have not's argue about their share of a pie cut into only a sliver. One heinous activity after the next. And here I am. Wondering what would be, if I was Eve.

He's Lost

He's lost
    Not knowing his capabilities
        Lost inside this community
           Of people he calls friends
Still driven by the peer pressure
    To not show his heart
        He is left bluffing
           Even when the game is long over.
He's lost
    Within himself
        Not knowing the depth or range
           Not knowing his ego or his own strange
           Habits.
He wants to develop
    Into a renaissance brother
        A man that holds himself to the highest
        standard
        If he could only stop lying to himself.
He still plays naïve
    It rips me, tears at me, drains me
        To sit back silently and watch
           His process of becoming a man.
What will it take to find him?

His Eyes

His eyes slant across the room
Like Roman shades
Peeled back
And emitting light
In the midst of gloom.
I see his thoughts play like reels
Of the most dramatic movie
As he moves me
With his silence.

He is the epitome of nonchalance
Not a beggar, a greeter
Not an activist, or thinker
Just existing…he is

He is hiding his chin in the palm
Of his hand as he watches
Me scrawl black ink
Across pure pages.
He must wonder,
Wonder why his light
Is only visible

By others.
The tint of his irises
Only allows him to see
Jaded views.

Skewed thoughts,
Tension in his heart
Shows across his face.
No stranger to Fate,
He prolongs his stare
Searching...
Hoping.

Excuses

The needle in my heart won't let me bleed
Because I tried to erase what I'd seen
I guess I'm a glutton for your love
Unrelenting.
Disregarding my intuition, my feelings
Just to find that
Crying only exhausts my body
My mind is still full and active
Replaying discussions like re-runs
Disbelief won't give me faith
To save our relationship
We missed.
Emotion in our kiss
Gone.
You lied on Fidelity and Truth
Abused my heart so heinously
With an excuse that you were
Losing love
Although not empty enough for you
To tell me, so
Who gives a fuck
About you being the fly caught in a web of lust?

Friend's Love

Many nights only delay the time I await
To move my hands over the edges of your face
And wonder why my hearts in the wrong place.
Friends we've been for so long
It seems eternity is our companionship
Because Love won't let us kiss.
We've been scared because of our audience.
It's made us distant
And somewhat tense
Separated by Fate's liaison
Destined to never try again.
Eyeing my moist lips
And curvy hips
In my pictures
Do you ever sit and figure
What could friends do for lovers?
Emotionally and physically in between the covers?
Fear has never stopped me
And those sleepy eyes and grin are luring
Me into sinful thoughts.
So I won't pretend
That I'm not falling in love with my friend.

Stranger

When I first glimpsed
That face from my dream
I must say
It was pristine
In image and structure
It punctured a heart valve
Made me calm
And sweaty-palmed
And nervous
To look too deeply
Into chocolate eyes
I'm seeping
And sinking
Deeper and deeper
Into a stranger's pores
Of his soul.
I begged for more
As he licked his lips
And crossed his fingertips
Into an embrace
That laced my spine
With invisible needles

And they lasted longer than a stranger's should.
I succumbed to his pull
Of my cerebral membrane
Played and frolicked
In the garden of his flowering mind
Plucked the roses of his deepest memories
And framed them
Labeled them
In a way that remained hidden to him.
He was a stranger to me
But I'd known him for too long.

Greeting to Remember

So you smiled when you saw her sitting
And was committing yourself
To walk in another direction
And had a self-reflection in that moment
You weren't scared
You could talk to any female
You said
To yourself in earnest
So you approached, offered your name
Sat down in the empty chair
That still swayed after the last man's attempt
You eyed her curvy body
Strong limbs attached to a sturdy frame
You surmised long rides,
Swimming the canal,
And propping those limbs atop yours
Not all at once unless she desired
Her smile belied the truth
She was indeed attracted to you
But she was a force to be reckoned with
You smirk, ask her about her dreams and wishes
All along the lines of whether she'd be submissive

When the time came
Would she let you take her to ecstasy
Unrestrained
She dips her head
In answer to your fleeting questions
Sips her drink with plump lips
You follow the swallow
Down the curve of her neck to her décolletage
To the mound of her full bust
Slowly rising and falling
Nipples taut.
You can't take it anymore
So you tell her:
I'm infatuated with you
You're beautiful
Not a prize to be won
But one to be cherished as such
I'd like to take you to a place you've never been
One we can't get to by car
A place not many have traveled or left
Will you come with me?

She takes your hand
A curiosity burning in her
Ready.

Book Report

Read me like a book
Don't worry about how the cover looks
Just know that there is substance inside
A plot to unfold
In your imagination behind your eyes
Let the story grip you
Hold you tight to the plotline
The way the words flow are like an instrumental
Symphonic and whispering to your soul
Don't flip through the intro page
And try to skim through an in depth novel
You could find yourself half way finished
And lost.
When you eyed the cover
Its brilliance and beauty took over
You knew it wasn't to be handled poorly
Hardbound, intellectual read
Finger the pages, take in the smell of its aged experience
Remember that each smudge is a reminder
Of those who have come before you
And have misplaced their valued original
Only to search for a copy.

Woman's Domain

Riding backseat to your dominance
Prominent in your mannerisms
Can I flip them?
And make them crave my supple breast
That you undress
With milk chocolatey eyes
As they roam towards my thighs
And I spin to show my spine
The black dress clinging to my skin
Are you getting the messages that I send?
Within our lustful minds, I beg you to
Grab my hips and twist
Me towards your firm chest
Nipple to nipple, breast to breast
Caress my glistening shoulder
Then we grind a little lower.
But I twist passed
As you try to take hold
I'm moving too fast
Trying to make you chase
I want this moment to last
Exhale as I raise my fingertips skyward

And you praise the Lord
For making a body like mine
That you will entwine
Tonight
In an hour's time
The club is still dim
As you fill my glass to the brim
And you watch me dance with him
Jealous but amused
By the sexual food
I've served on the dance floor
You eye my tanned, glistening arms
As they curl seductively to the music
And I use it
To point a finger to you and curl it towards my palm
Stay calm
As you enter the woman's domain.
Wild, exotic and untamed.

Thank Remembrance

Love exists in your toothy grin
At my humorless lines of inexperience
Yet, again and again
You make me feel
Surreal in my comedic talents.
Many nights you saved me from the witch
That haunted my bedside
Or laughed when I fell on the Slip-N-Slide.
How many times have you pretended?
Pretended to be frightened
Or enlightened by my creativity
Even when it was a ghastly tree ornament
Or a scary story I would tell
But in love you fell
With my bright eyes that begged for a smile
Or giggle from the back of your throat
Remember the hurt?
The pain of me stepping into the corridor
Of an airplane
All alone but you prayed for me, didn't you?
It may sound insane but
I heard you.

I recollect the dookie braids
Or the too sweet lemonade
I remember laying in your bouncy bed
With adolescent stories streaming from my head
And you listened…
I felt those tears in my hair as I cried
Or the glance when I brought home
Lace underwear, thinking I was adult enough
I've grown
And all the while
I've known no love greater than that of my father.

Forever Hold Your Peace

You wanted to surprise me with a kiss
Across the tender, wettest part of my lips
But you didn't.
You wanted to love me
But sheered by intimidation
You succumbed to your own humiliation.
For letting something slip
Through buttered fingertips
So valued and loved by you
To only leave yourself with dreams
That gleam like stars in your memory
And you will hate the next time you see me
Because I embody every dream you dreamt
Each time the pillow dented as you slept
There are no second chances.

Ease the Tension

I need you
    Right now
       Right here
        In my arms.
Erase the fear
    Of loneliness
       That clouds me more
        And more each day.
Lay
    Your arms around my body
       Ease the tension
        In my shoulder.
Hold me longer
    Than you ever have
       I'm doomed to fall into your trap
        Mesmerized.
Yes, I've fantasized
    About you between my thighs
       So ease the tension
        Massage away the doubt.
Soothe me into forever.

Words

Will the words I speak
Even reach you?
Today, tomorrow, next week?
Will you truly understand
The perplexity of my posture
On things unbeknownst to me?
I keep
Thinking things
Will be explained in greater detail
Yet they still remain
Sitting on the desk, in the darkened
Chambers of your mind.
Held captive by the cowardly guard
Called Pride
I wish to know you deeply
Wish to touch your innermost
Private parts
Those things hidden
Cloaked in shame
Never revealed.
These are the things I wish to feel
Understand and cling to.

So my words, meaningless as they are
Only hope to define why my brow
Etches a face of discontented confusion.
So my smile is only
My demeanor lacking the mask.
I wish to know the words
That will cut you open
And let you bleed your wisdom on me
Because I am
Thirsty for more
More of you.

Hindsight

Confused on the best route to take
Wondering if I will or have
Made a mistake
Wanting so much to be mature
So ready and willing
But only faced with pressure
Squeezing me down
Holding me back from being 100% happy
Hoping that time will heal old wounds
That were swept away with the sting of truth
Lacking the cocoa butter to fade it
But gradually I've made it by
Picking old scars to see if they will bleed
Or hurt like the first time.
All the while…crying.
Painful self-inflicted blows
To the heart, the chest
My mind, esteem, my dreams
Stifled.
Slowly suffocated beneath
Responsibility.
And fear of loss

Fear of trust.
When you've been hurt so deeply
You never forget the wound
Or how it felt to you.
The memory lingers
On the tip of every conversation
Or argument disguised as a discussion
I balled up my self-respect
And shot it to the wastebaskets
Just to find out that I needed it later.

Cherish

I cherish the scent of him
The smile that hides
Beneath his lying eyes
"We are just friends"
An unspoken bond
Aching for more
Of what lacks in our crippled relationship.
We exist between nothingness
And everything.
I still sing
His praises in my quiet time
And smile idly to stop the cries
Because I miss feeling like the only one
The only being that matters
In this crazy world.
I missed the mental and emotional kiss
As it all became so twisted
So quick.
Now distant memories cloud me
In the darkness of my bedroom
The past invades me
The memory of

His sensuality and passion
Are unforgiving as I caress my womanly essence
And sigh to the release
It reminds me of heaven
Or what it would be like.
I cherish the memory
Of when I was someone
Special.

Melon-choly

If I could open my mind
Like a juicy melon
And allow you to ingest
The intelligence
Or prove my sweetness
By letting you taste
The succulence of my tenderness
Squish my soft, ooey gooey places
Places no one has ever seen
Or taken for granted
If I could slice a piece of me
Away from the ripe core of me
I would let my filling drip
From the tip of your chin
As you tongue the excess of me
Clean
Until there is nothing left
But seeds.

Leftovers

I keep opening the leftovers of our relationship
Shame, I want something so picked over
Old, and
Funky
We have fun together
Laughing beneath soiled covers
Swearing to each other
We are here to stay
But that was months ago
Before drama and boredom were the headline play
Now I'm in the audience
As you do the same old song and dance
Hoping that I'll look your way
But your obvious attempt to sway my opinion
Is unreceived…at the moment.
This is the time when my mind
Starts doing cartwheels into the past
I'm remembering the last kiss, last touch
Last lick, last fuck
And yes, it was *that* good.
Good enough
To make me want you more

And more

Until you couldn't go anymore

Sadly, we've been down this road before

And like always

With a little heat…

Who doesn't like leftovers?

Relating to the Worst in Us

Frustrated with the way life serves trials
He squints his eyes
Scrunches his brows
And in his glare, speaks of sorrow.
Things he doesn't own,
Repayment of what's borrowed
No results, no returns
Just giving to be generous
Never receiving appreciation
Lonely, desolate young man
With the world rolling in the palm of his hand
But he can't hold it tight
Just hoping that his fist remains closed
Wrapping the world tight
Putting injustice on pause
He still speaks.
His baritone voice taking me to peaks
Of understanding
I feel his trouble
I warrant his anger
Knowing how it feels to be popular
In a world of strangers

Everyone out to see him fall
Hopeless, helpless beneath
Skies of hope and help into the darkness
Yet like tar, he slowly oozes his way forward
His forehead creased, breath increased
Dreams deceased
I feel him.
His anger like water that leaks, turning
Something so small into something so large
He quenches me like a limeade drink
And yes, we think on the same plain.
I'm grazing the homeland to the wasteland
Picking his comfort zone to engage emotion
And we float together
Ravishing our memories, seeing anger more clearly
He lets it step out in the open
Be free of all restraints
Forced to be ourselves
Free to relate
He still looks deeply but his eyes have cleared
And brows unraveled
Lips un-pursed, now smirked
And he looks deeply still but not in anger…
Only in relief.

Are We There Yet

How did we get here?
Far from home
Stranded
And starving for emotional restraint
We dived too deep
Into the sea
Of the unknown
Its black curls like suds
Hiding its depths
We keep gasping for air
Hoping there's
One more breath
Just enough to keep us afloat
And fighting for more
I've fallen beyond the level
Of my expertise
I've sunk to the bottom
Of the bottomless
And never hit rock.
How did we get here?
A leaf hanging on to the only thing left
The branch bent by forceful winds

The odds against us
The fear in us
Of falling
Keeps us rooted in our own ways
How did we get to the point
Where pleasure and pain mixed,
Coagulated and created a crust
Of nonchalance and jealously.
Are we there yet?

Fall of Succession

Silly thoughts emit light to dim understanding
So what happens when the light goes out?

I'm in the wind
Like leaves in Fall
Still tumbling along
Down an unknown path
Hoping I get there sooner
Than my first crack
Or crumble under society's shoe
I'll re-emerge from the stem
Forced to die and start all over again.
I have to succeed.
     I have to succeed.
          I have to succeed.

For the Lonely Ones

Silent but not quiet
Hearing but unheard
Knowing the answer but not the words
Always right but feels so wrong
A yearn for more
So weak, it's strong

This is for the lonely ones
The tempted ones
The princesses of lost love.
Un-held hearts and hands
That yearn so deeply for a man
But not suffering the work it takes
Who's to blame?
It's a continuous cycle
That begins and ends the same.

This is for the lonely ones
On rainy nights, depression filtering
Sleepless, weakness undrained
That never seems to end
The lonely ones

Frank, twisted in imaginary reality
But all are made by the bones of two structures
Crossed in passionate juxtaposition
Easy, stressless, confident, refreshing...
Manipulation.

Music

Caramel chocolate, sweet brown
Hovers above ground
Towards the music box
Long fingers spin the record
Release the arm and silence is interrupted
Captured by bass drums
And soft acapella hums
As I watch the silk tighten
Against massive mounds of taut flesh
Your body, the hills and valleys
Of Egyptian pyramids and Mayan ruins
Fluent in your motion
Each step the beat of a different drum
It must be the music
As it swirls around in gentle winds
And soon turns to violent storms
Don't grip my arm
And pull me to your face!
Grind into me, hand tight on my waist
I can't take this…
Pleasure.
Music fills me, trembles
Shaking me with underground tones
Just once, let me not get taken by the music.

Receipts to Keep

They say relationships are like games
But who volunteered me to play?
I don't recall ever asking to be heartbroken
Or used as a token, stamped with a picture
Of his beautiful women.
I just wanted innocent love
The kind where you don't have to sucker
The next man into a twisted game
Of what's falsely true
While they hide how much they want to use you
I thought I was the strongest
Toughest
Down-right roughest girl
On the southern edge of Lake Michigan
But this man ripped my intent
Into ragged shards of receipts
Receipts used to get back to me
To come back because he knew love was there
Still waiting
On layaway
Still debating
On if it was unfair

Or degrading to be pulsating at his entrance
Or teary-eyed at his disagreements
I was undoubtedly the pawn in his game
Admittedly, I do mind
Because what I let slip by this time
Will only come back to haunt me.

The You I Knew

We sigh beneath evening's velvety blue
I heard a mistake in your voice
As we converse, late
You don't move me
Like you used to do me
You don't understand
What your body's poetry
Tries to sing to me
But your lips are pursed tight
Psss…
Your eyes looking in the distance
Missing the instant
I switch from bright to dim.
On a whim
We started this thing
Vowing to have no chains
Just links
That tie us together
Loosely
Now we have something
So confusing,
So filled with delusions

Of how we think we are

And how things are supposed to be

Or like I thought they were.

Between temper tantrums and sarcasm,

I don't understand your motivation

Yet elation still fills my body

Nourished, when you give me

A moment in eternity.

A slave

I would be, if allowed

But I'm chasing

A man, mentally

But physically, he's unwilling to distort things

With the release of my nectar

Mixed with his passion fruit

We make a dish worth savoring.

So no longer do I pursue.

I let you

Do what you feel you should do

And here we are…

Effortless.

Parted.

Undeniably unhappy

With not knowing.

Cat won't chase dog

If dog is to lead cat
I'm still looking for the importance
Of the future with you.
Show me
What to look forward to
Tell me
What you wish to hold close
I miss you
The you I used to know.

Educational Sex

Put your books down
No more work
I announce with a sexy smirk.
You release *The Great Gatsby* on the wooden table
And eye the label
Knowing you should study to not fail
But my gaze is luring you away
Further from the bindings of the book
And deeper into my sexual look.
I grab your hand and
You unbend your knees to follow
Through the empty library
Pass the books on fairies, rows on war
And we stop at the darkest corner
I open a book on Kama Sutra
As you laugh aloud
I scan the marked page…proud and ready
Forcefully, you are pushed into the rack
And my tongue attacks your neck
Your nipples beneath your shirt
Pushed high over your head
Revealing your tautness

Your moans fill the silent building instantly
And you attempt to caress me
But I refuse
And continue
Opening your jeans, zipper down
A slice of sound in the emptiness
Sweet seduction, moans as I suction
My lips to your ear lobe
Hand probing lower
I twist you into every position highlighted
And you breathe heavily as if frightened
Small shivers then a shake
You've taken all you can take
And release into the dark quiet
Give me all that drips from you.
As we walk back to our table
We think about our brief break
And seem to relive how
We wondered from our work
Back to the dark corner
Fulfilling and educating simultaneously.

Woman

Silver bangled wrists, twisting hips
Catching every eye…female and male
Caught in a stare
Beautiful temptress with rhythmic nonchalance
Uncaring and free
Made of the finest, richest red dirt
Her mind is paid all that it's worth
There's no need to court
A stallion from the wilderness
Driven by an ambitious pilot
Twisting through curves of turbulence
Just to roll and continue smooth flight
Her faced welcomed in sunlight
Helps cure society's sleepless nights
Just to live curiously through her poetry

Her words like sweet pound cake
Finished with cool milk to a famished face
Thirsty
Thirsty for her knowledge
Thirsty for her intelligence beyond college
She quenches and makes you full

Her body filled like a meadow in Spring
Her stride like a honeybee preparing to sting
It's victim...
Slow motion until your surprise!
Ha! She's the seafowls, the Earth's crust
She suckled off Mother Nature's bust
To feed perfection
To feed the attraction
She's detangled, chainless and she'll always remain
this...
Riveting
Spellbinding
Woman.

Sexual Offerings

So you have my body, now tell me this
Caress all the places you want to kiss
Your tongue slithering down my crevices
And we fumble around in a manner so careless
A glimpse at your wild sex at its peak
As I fell your hands on my cheeks
I'm off the ground and on a vertical incline
Iniquitous fantasies attack my mind
Our bodies entwine…
The love is more passionate and incredulous
The warmth of our bodies connecting us
Unbelievable is this sexual episode
As you release the tension and explode
Your sweat drips and tickles my breast
Then you release me and start getting dressed
Useless and tainted, I gather my spirit
I asked you to stay but you wouldn't hear it
Once again, I'm not stimulated but abused
My mind, body and soul tragically used
It's not your fault; I dealt this hand
For offering my body to an undeserving man.

The Yearn

Passion unfolds as his nakedness enters
Lights dim, music playing, body tender
Night is overdue, waited for this day
As he grips my shoulders
Massages my neck, down to my navel
Past my treasures
Declining is no longer available
As he pulls me to the floor
Undressing slowly, all the while talking
Speaking of my beauty and elegance
He spreads my legs
Knees pressing them further apart
His hands search my temple
For my ripe nipples with soft lips, wet tongue
When he finds what he wants
He pursues his desires
Between my thighs
Emotions intensified, body hot, mind high
Rhythm moves my hips, grinds into him
His manhood unquestionable
Pounding hearts touch through heated skin
Perspiration beads on his forehead

As he changes the game plan

He slithers downward

Grabs the meat of my rear

And the sounds are barely there

As he arches my back, pulls me close

And in one motion, circles his tongue

And as I froze…

He follows the trail to the forest

Pulls it taut and caresses the wetness

The jumping in my thigh involuntary

The rush only momentary

Until the next, and the next, and then the next

He slurps the button, nibbles the lips

And flicks his juicy mass against the tenderness

My breathing stops, my mind blanks

Hoping it never finishes

But feeling it coming to a crescendo

My leg locked around his back, enclosing him

He moves me further up on the floor

Until I surround his warmth

Gathering him inside my warm, slick canal

His moans make it final

No more to learn

We are surrounding each other and

Satisfying the yearn.

Pina Colada

We existed in whirlwinds
He was always telling me I'm wrong
Because he liked to fight
I was always claiming I'm right
Because I like passionate sex at night
He was the epitome of man
Had bad points
But none too difficult to withstand
Most people watched us
Because they weren't used to
Black and Caucasian
Existing in whirlwinds, we were
Sleepless in the night's eye
We talked, we loved and fought
But I could never shake
The idea of me selling out
So I caused confusion.
Tried to corrupt a good thing
Because life ain't worth living
Without love
But love can't survive without
Something more

Something like dedication and acceptance.
My peers never made me breakfast
Or massaged my back with African oils
So why was I so devoted
To destroying a good thing
I tried to make sense of nonsense
By saying we were so…*different*
Weren't we?
He liked to make a list to the go to the store
And wash his car in his good shoes
And I used all these bullshit lines
To push him away
Just to crave the smell of his aftershave
And get angered at the empty closet space
I let those who could give a damn
About if I succeed or fail
Tell me who to love
And how to be ashamed
But see, we existed in whirlwinds
So I gave definition to
Once you go black, you never go back
And called him.
As I lay in bed with
Broken glass over black and white pictures
Hoping he'll ask me to come back

Say he missed my presence, my love and
My essence
His voice came through static
Static that wasn't the phone
We weren't...connecting.
I wasn't understanding
His version of things
He said he cried three nights
And only two he could sleep
So I apologized
And he recognized
The sound of a woman led astray
I envisioned cigarette butts, full ashtrays
Old food on TV trays
As he waits, for my call...
But I was wrong
And he was so right.
So I asked to come over
He said meet him halfway
So I stumbled under streetlights
In pajama pants and house shoes
He was there
Looking less confused
Then I envisioned he would
I saw the white skin

But within
I saw a soul burnt,
A heart scarred
And as we closed the gap
On slick streets
We let lips meet in apology.

Other Books by T.R. Horne

Contemporary Romantic Suspense
Breaking Mobius - Available NOW

Mystery/Suspense
Girl Soldier - Available NOW

Dystopian Suspense Trilogy
The Unmasked Nation: The Upper Guild (Book One) - 2017
The Unmasked Nation: Schizm Division (Book Two) - 2018
The Unmasked Nation: Junta (Book Three) - 2019

Flash Fiction (eBook only)
Crazy Dirty Love (Second Edition) - 2017

Stay in touch by following T.R. Horne on Twitter, Facebook and Instagram @Authortrhorne
Check out T.R. Horne at www.trhorne.com

About the Author

T.R. Horne is an avid reader, reviewer and all around critic of things written and not written (just ask her poor husband). She writes suspense novels for the most part but flirts with her first love, Poetry, from time to time. Between studying for her doctorate and dreaming of retiring early and moving into a tiny house, she carries on with a pretty lackluster life filled with a 9-5 job, sore feet and a perpetual smile. She resides in Virginia but calls Atlanta, Georgia home when people ask. Thank her husband, son and two dogs for keeping her mildly sane and writing.